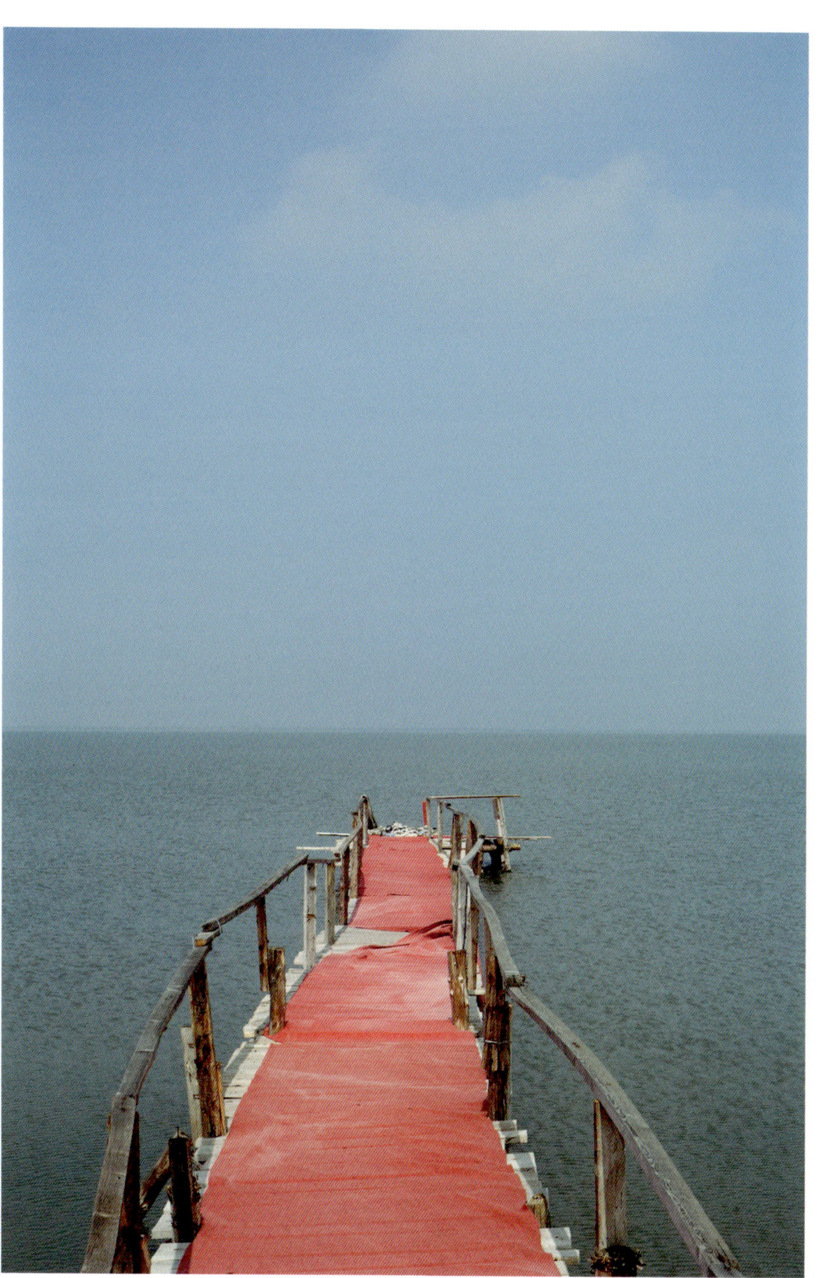

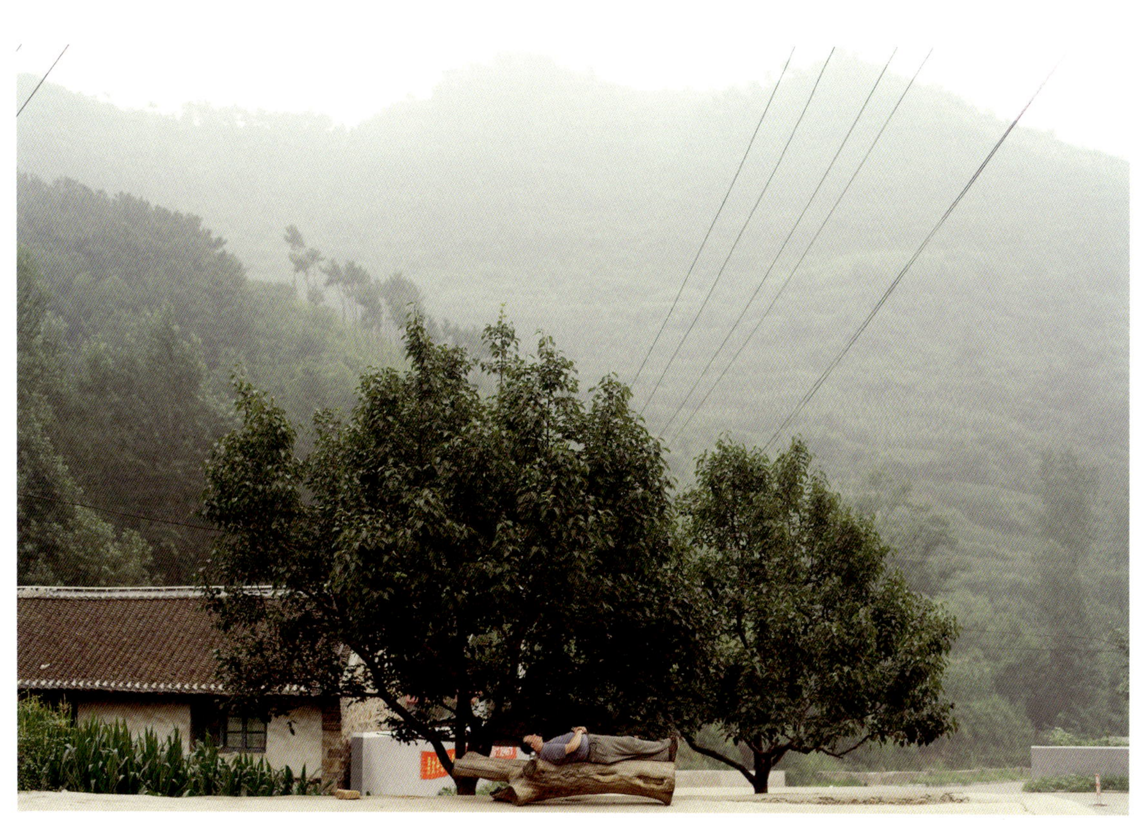

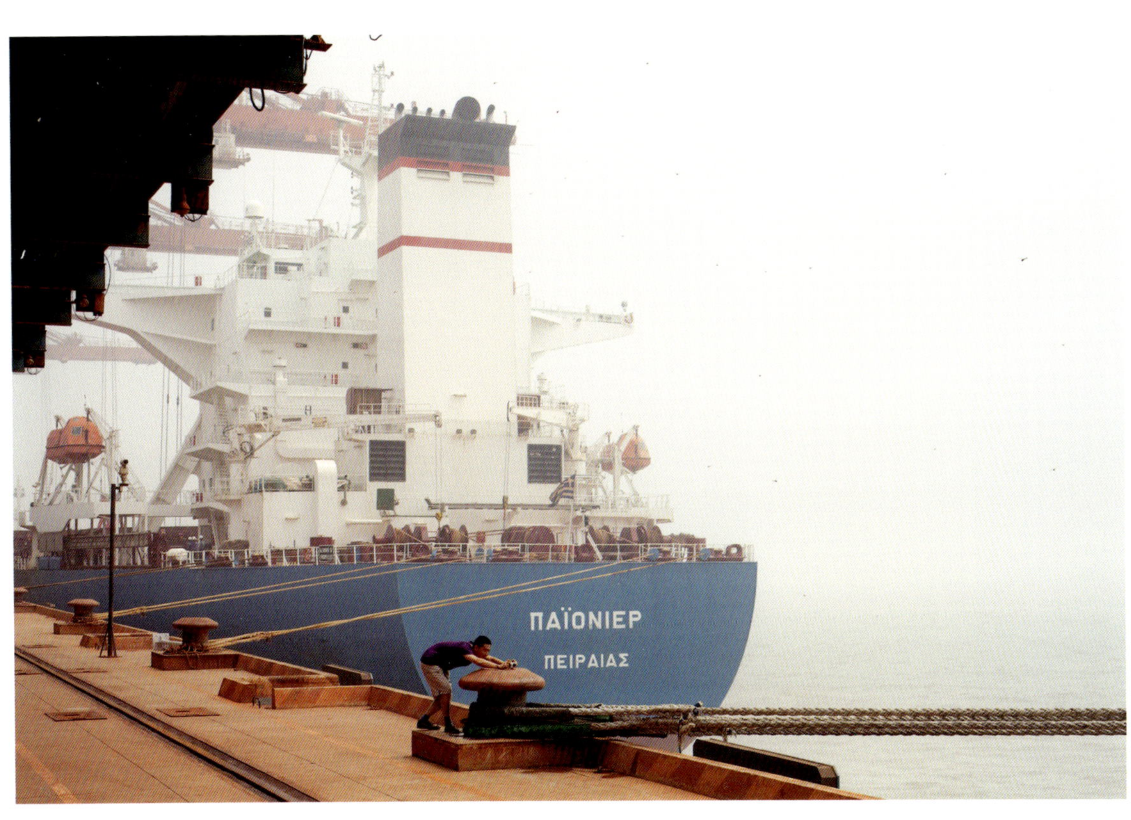

ΠΑΪΟΝΙΕΡ
ΠΕΙΡΑΙΑΣ

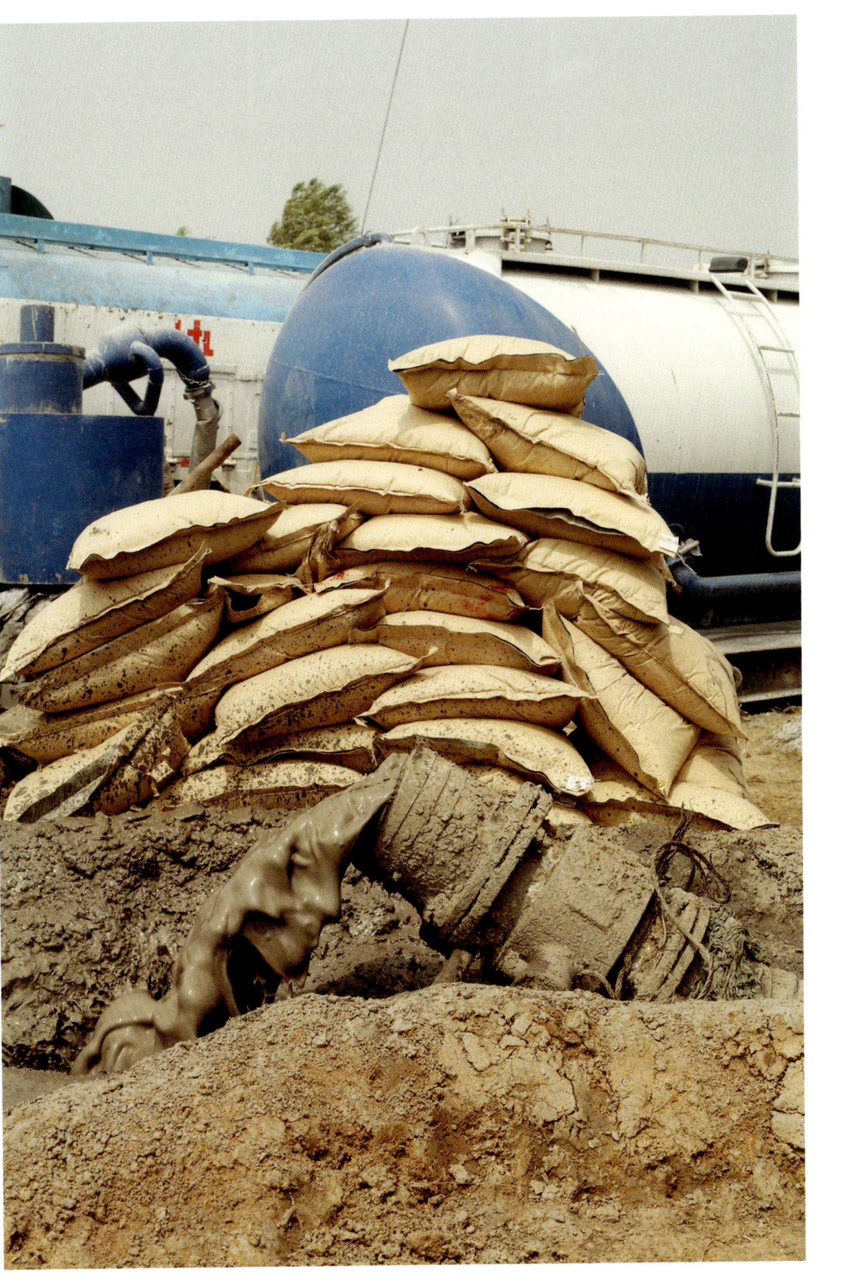

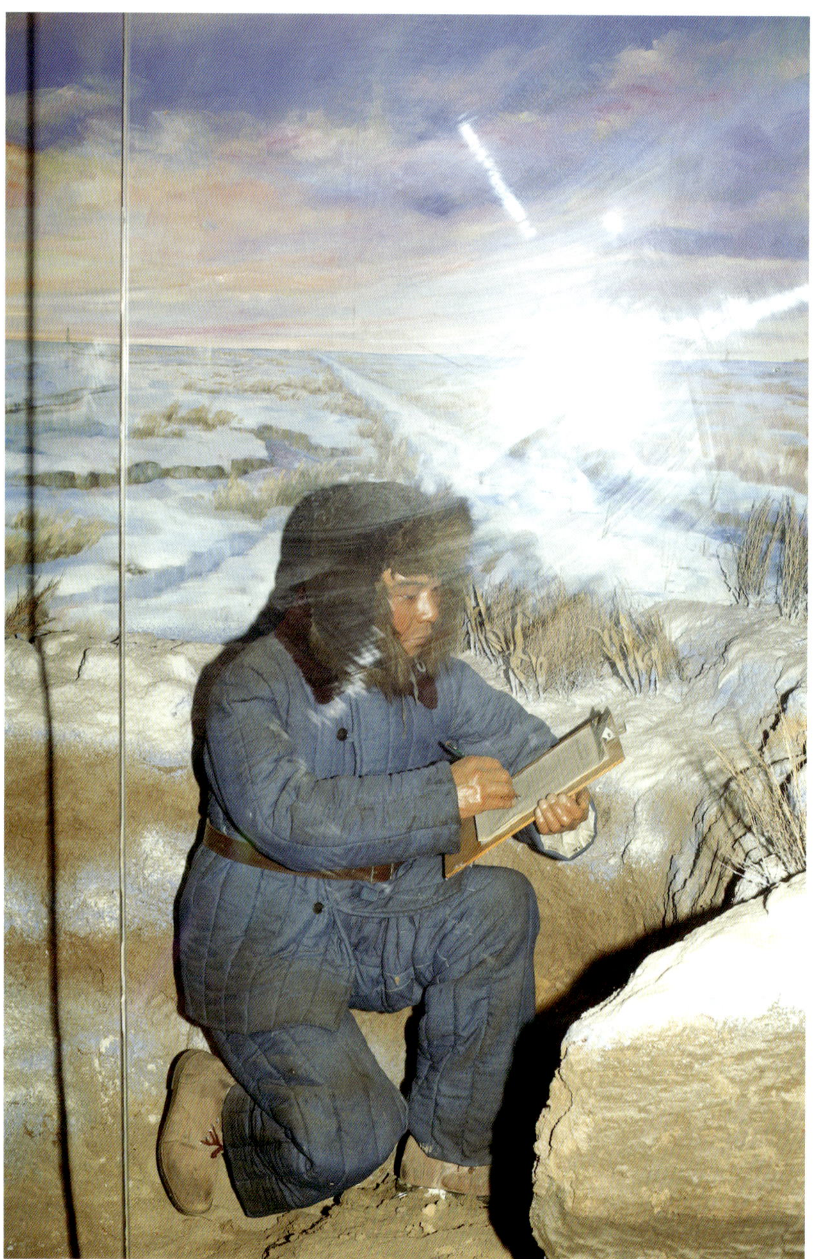

SHAWN RECORDS   **FROM THE BOTTOM OF A WELL**

A-JUMP BOOKS

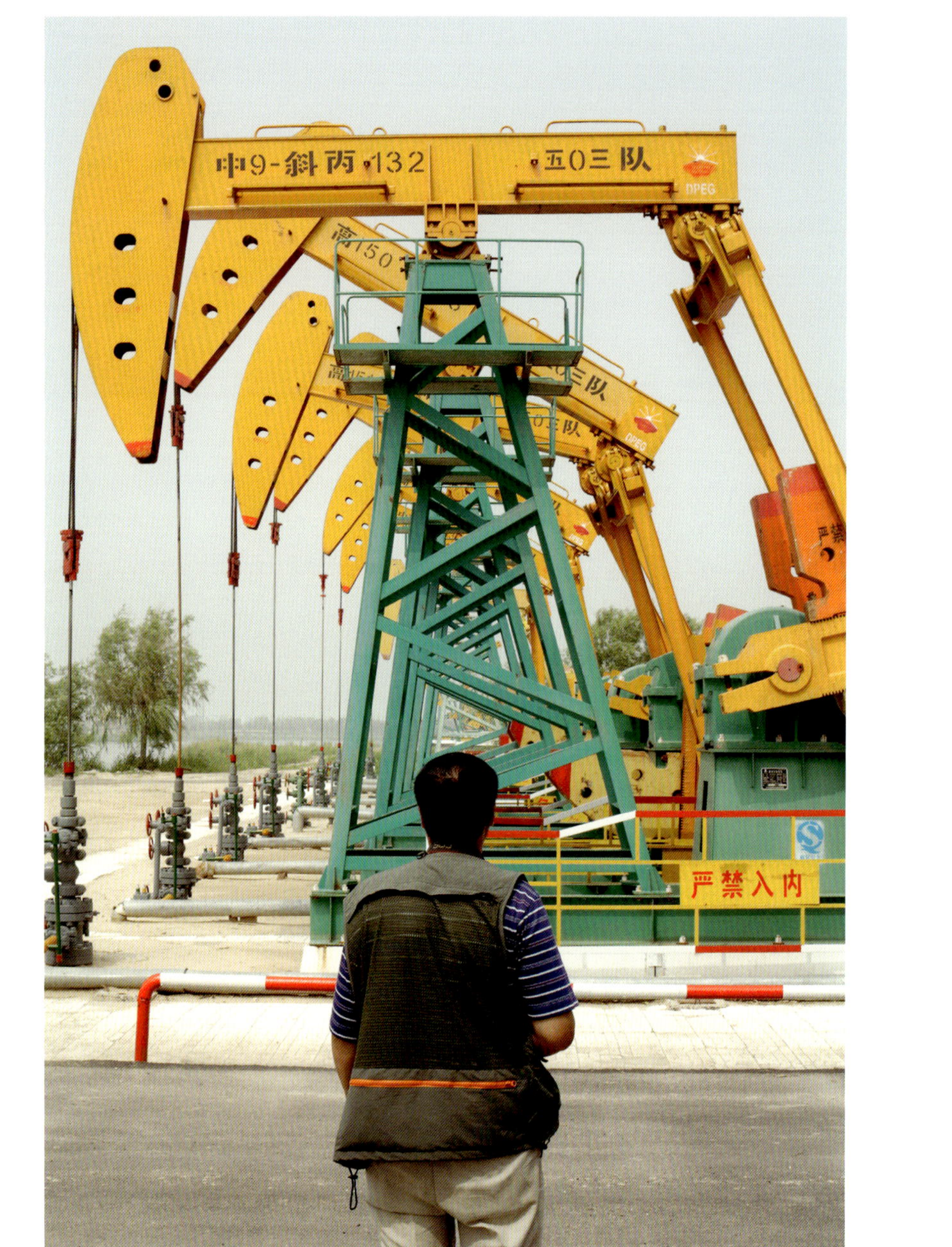

中9-斜丙-132
五〇三队
DPEG
严禁入内

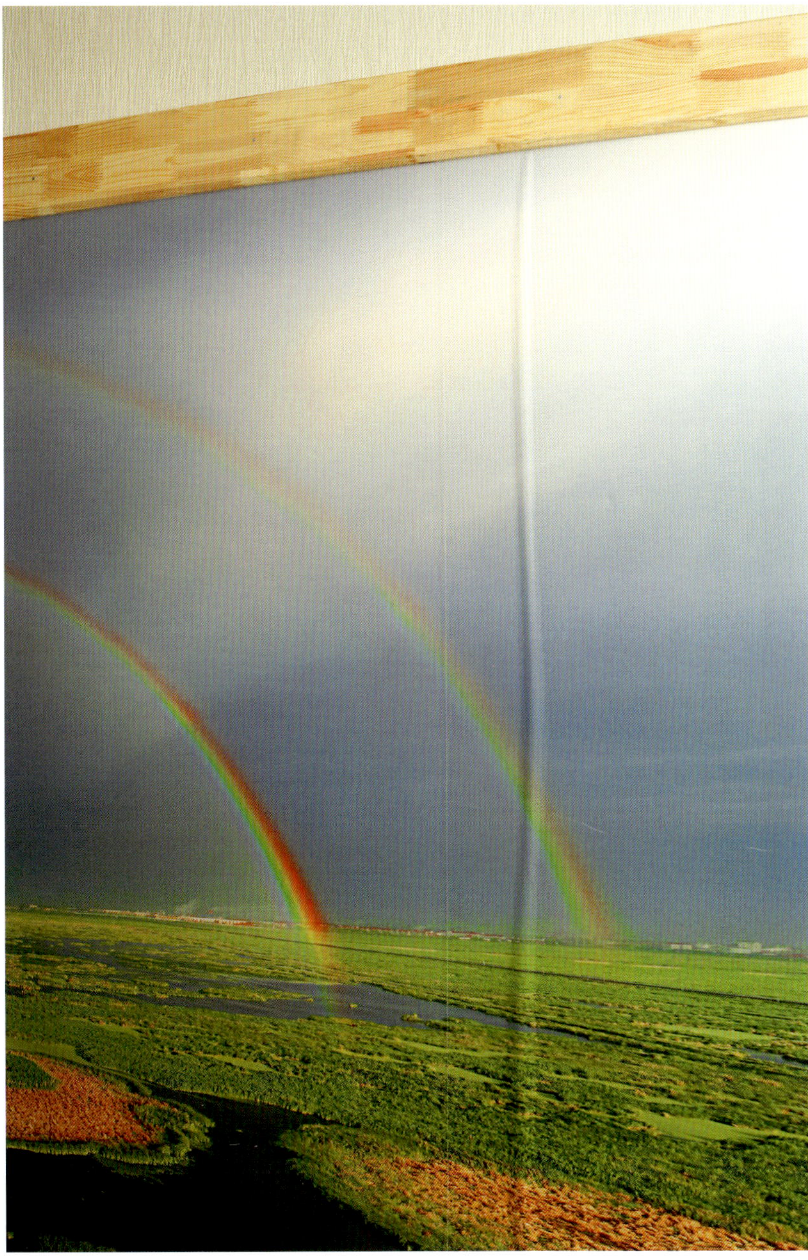

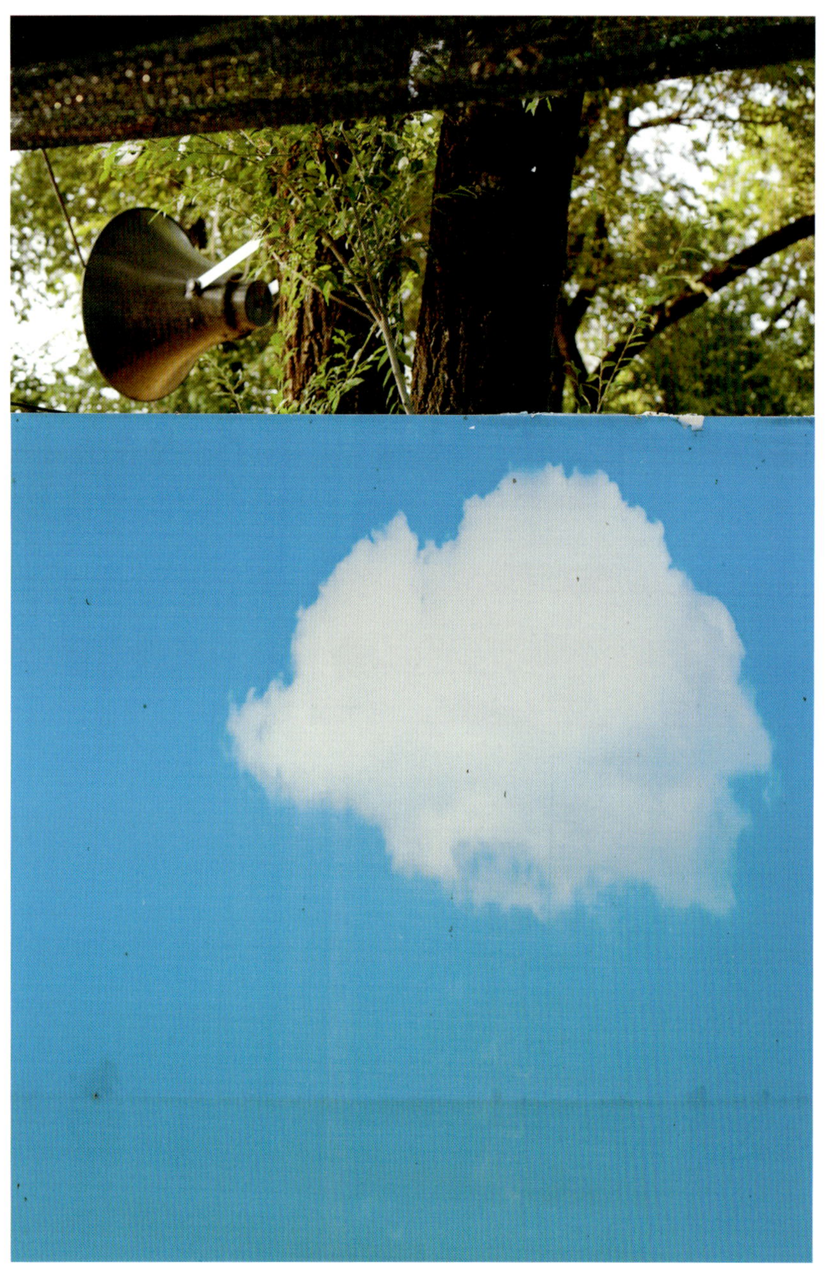

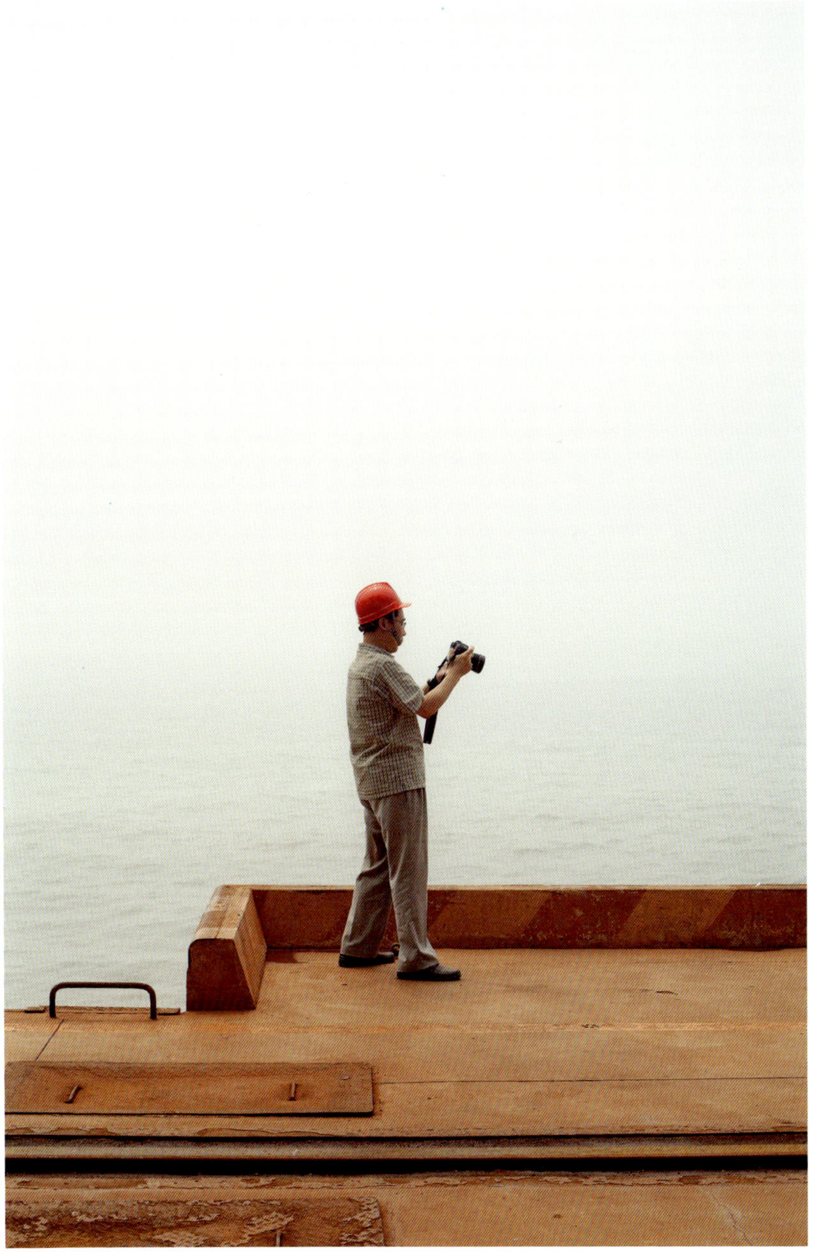

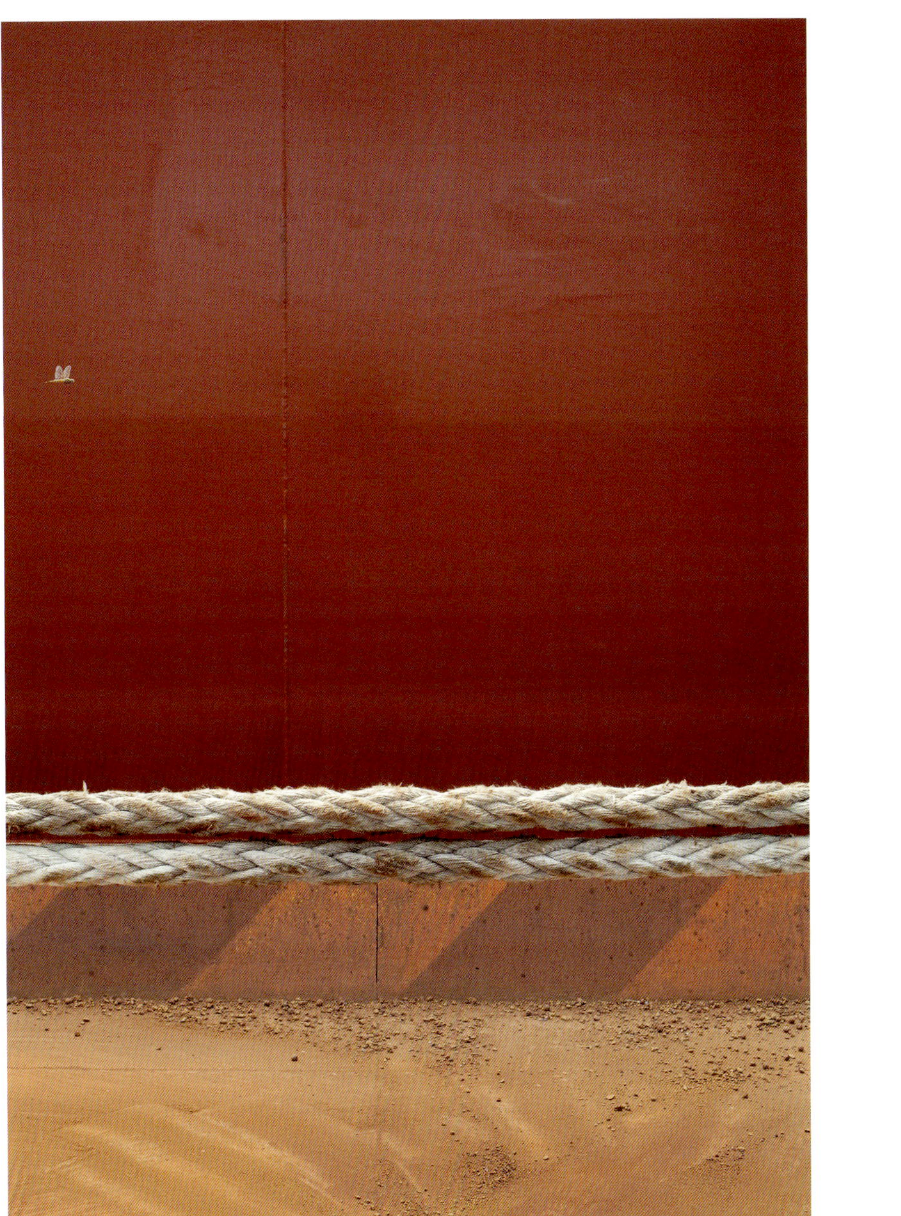

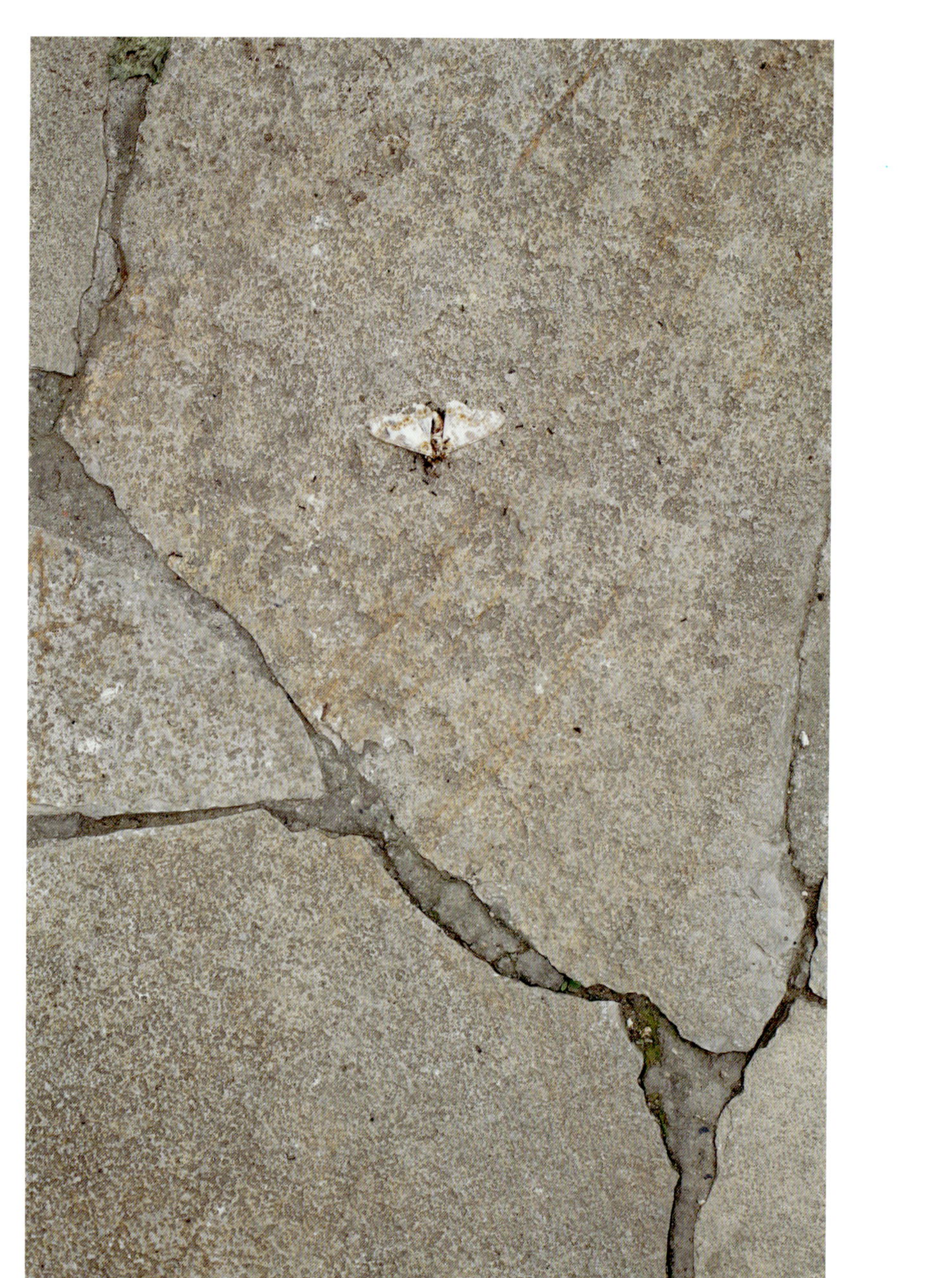

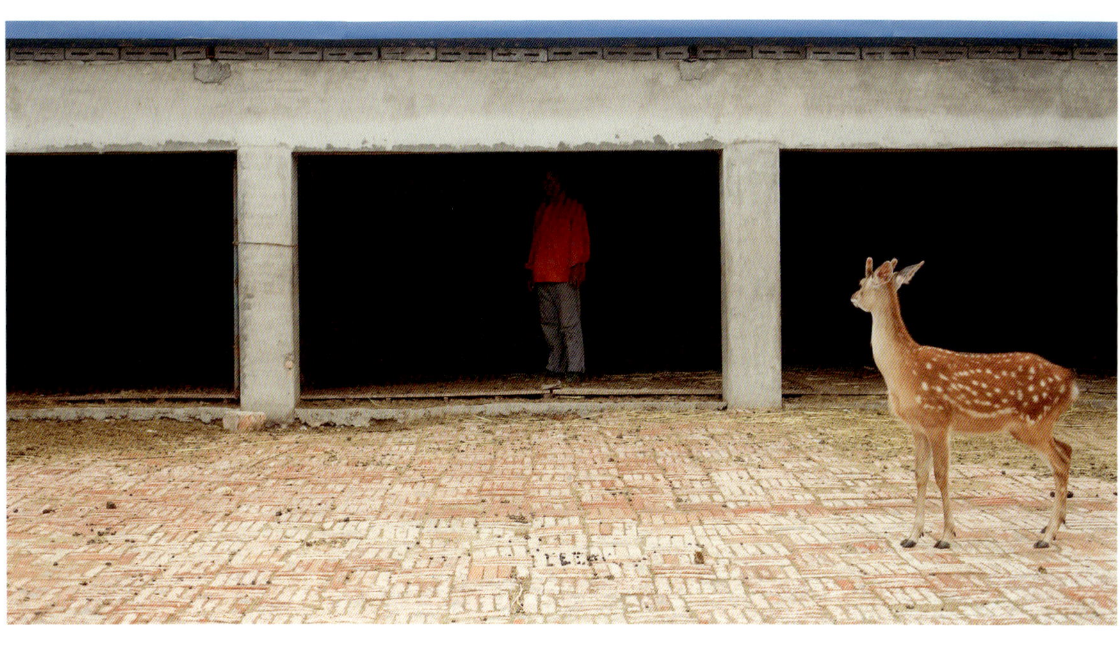

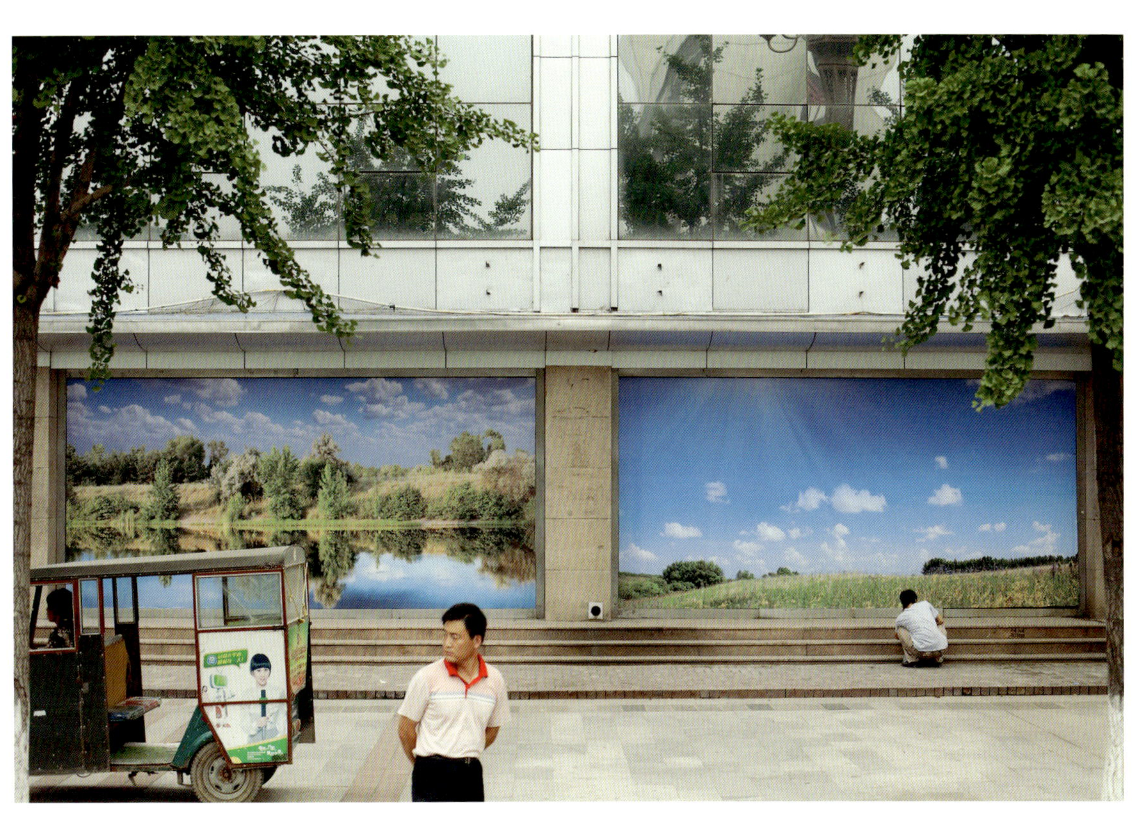

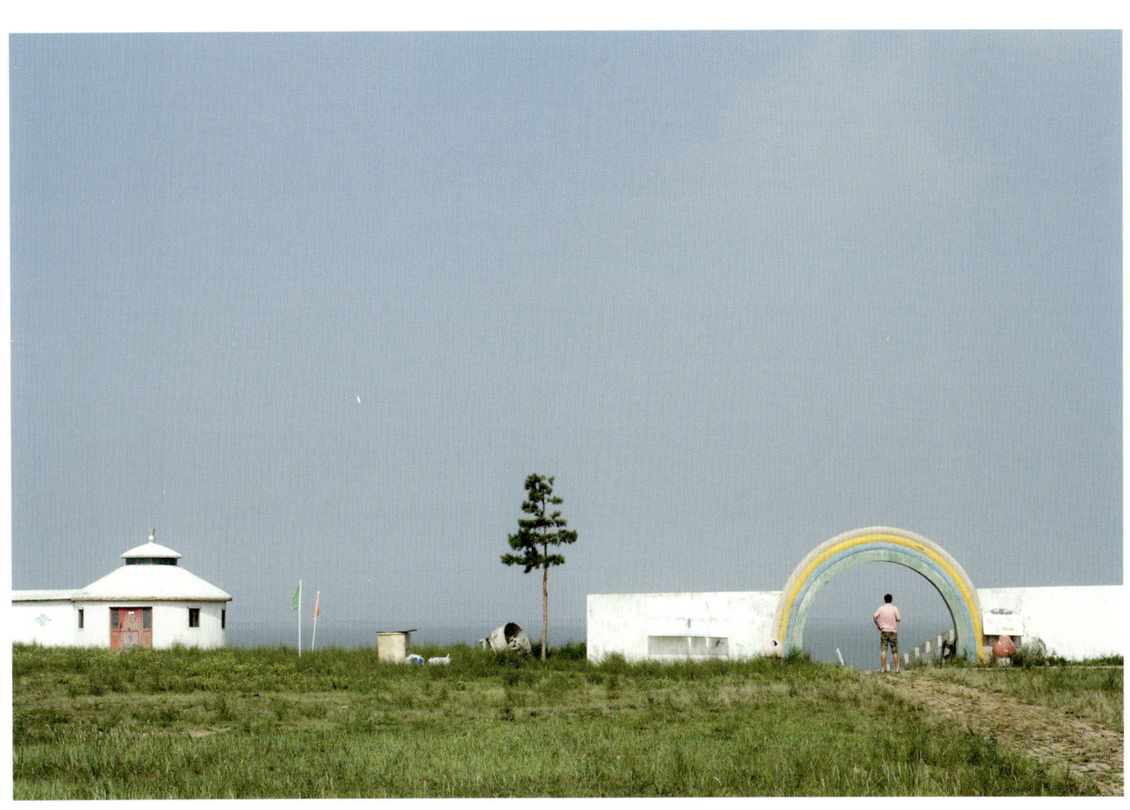

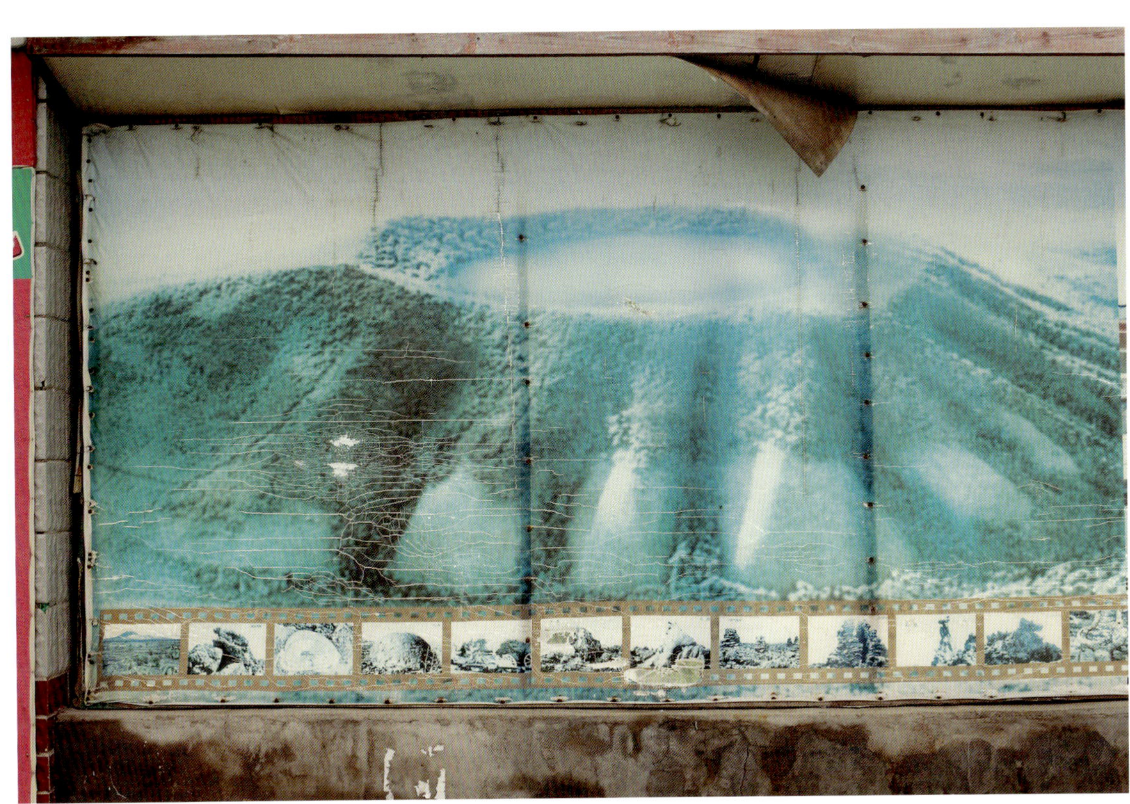

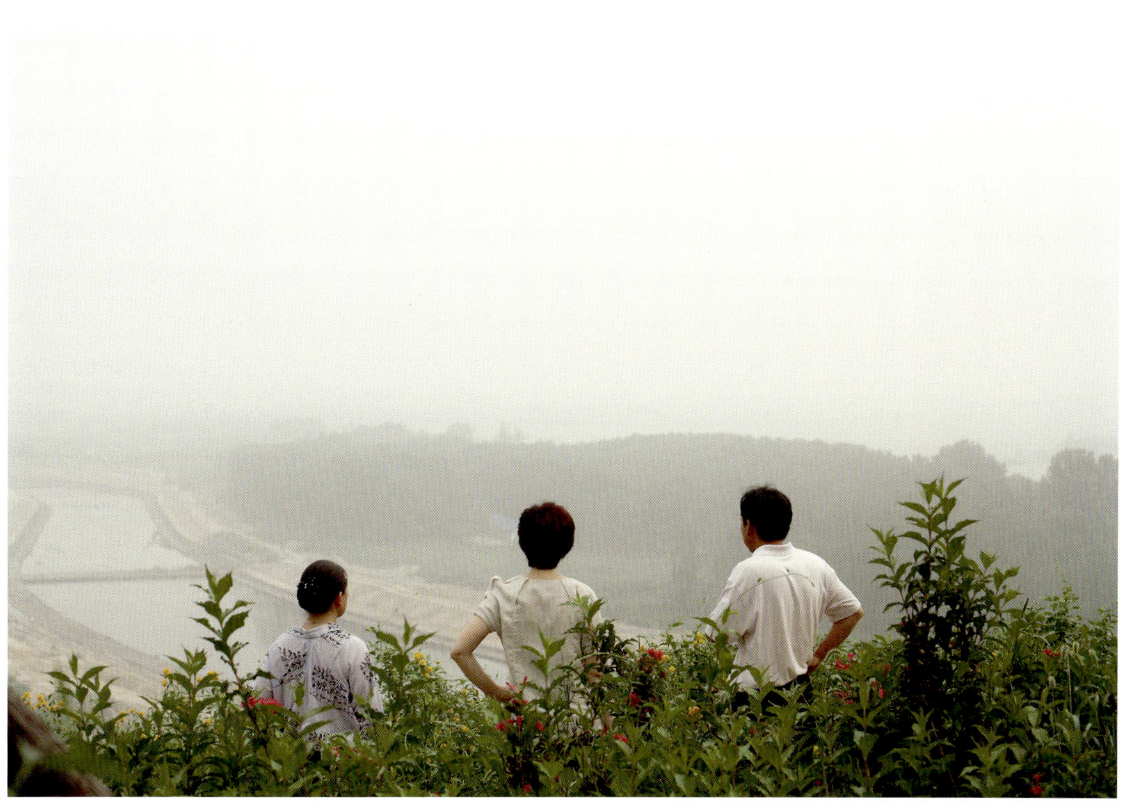

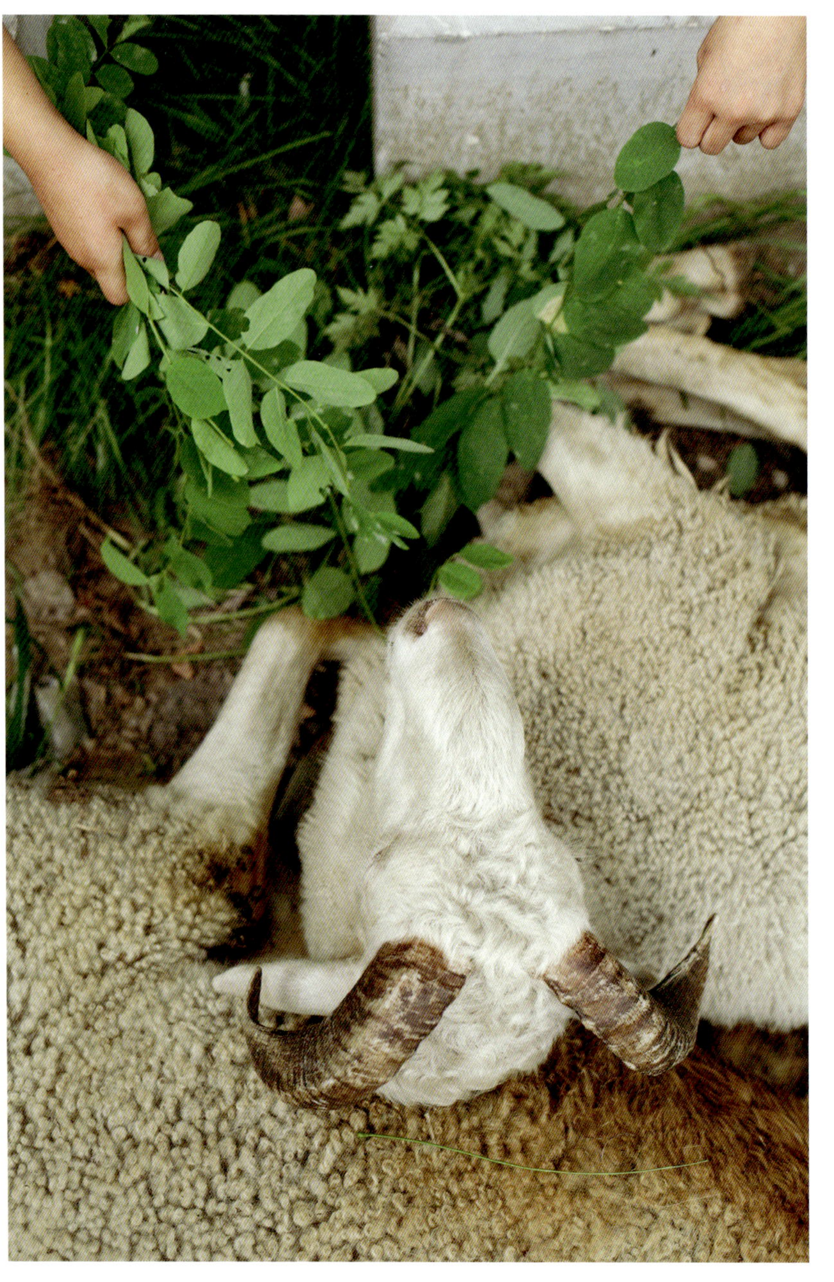

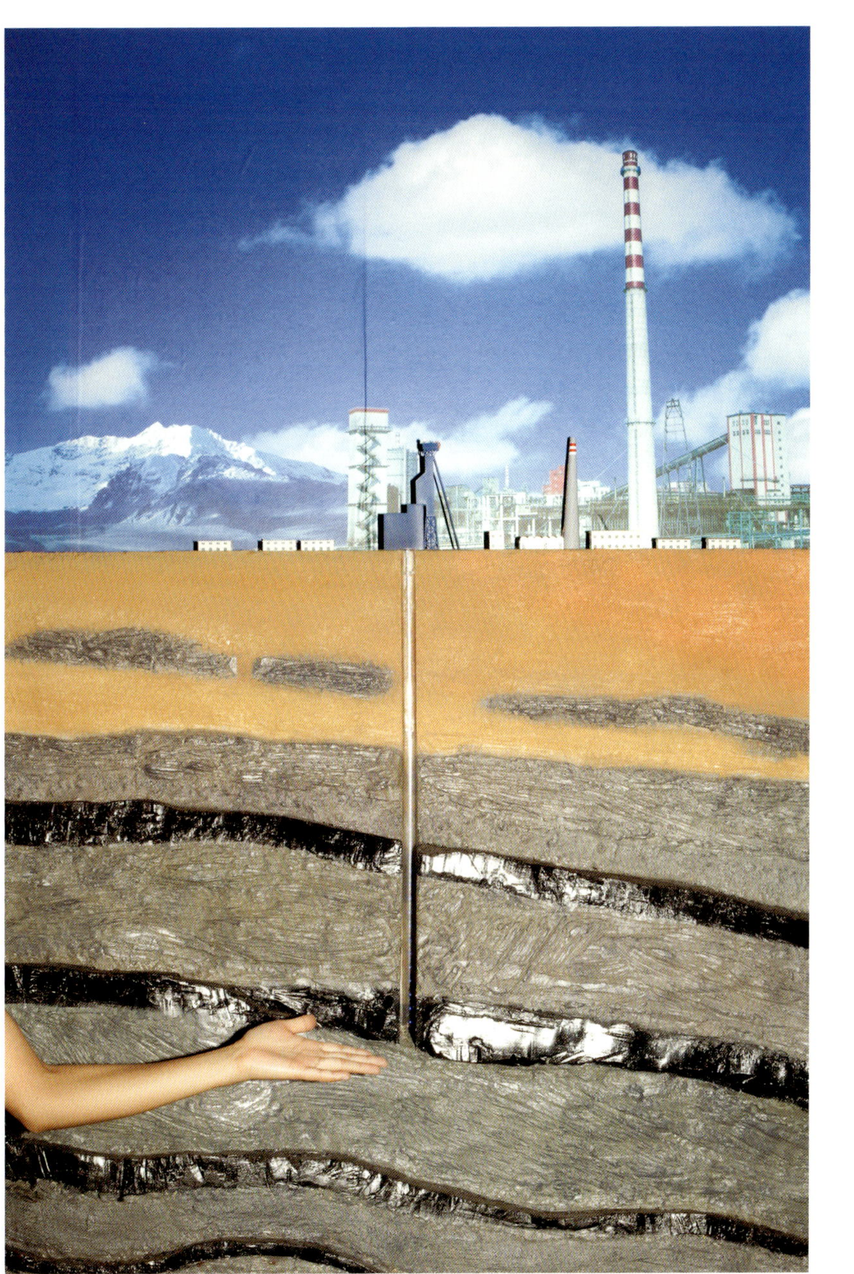

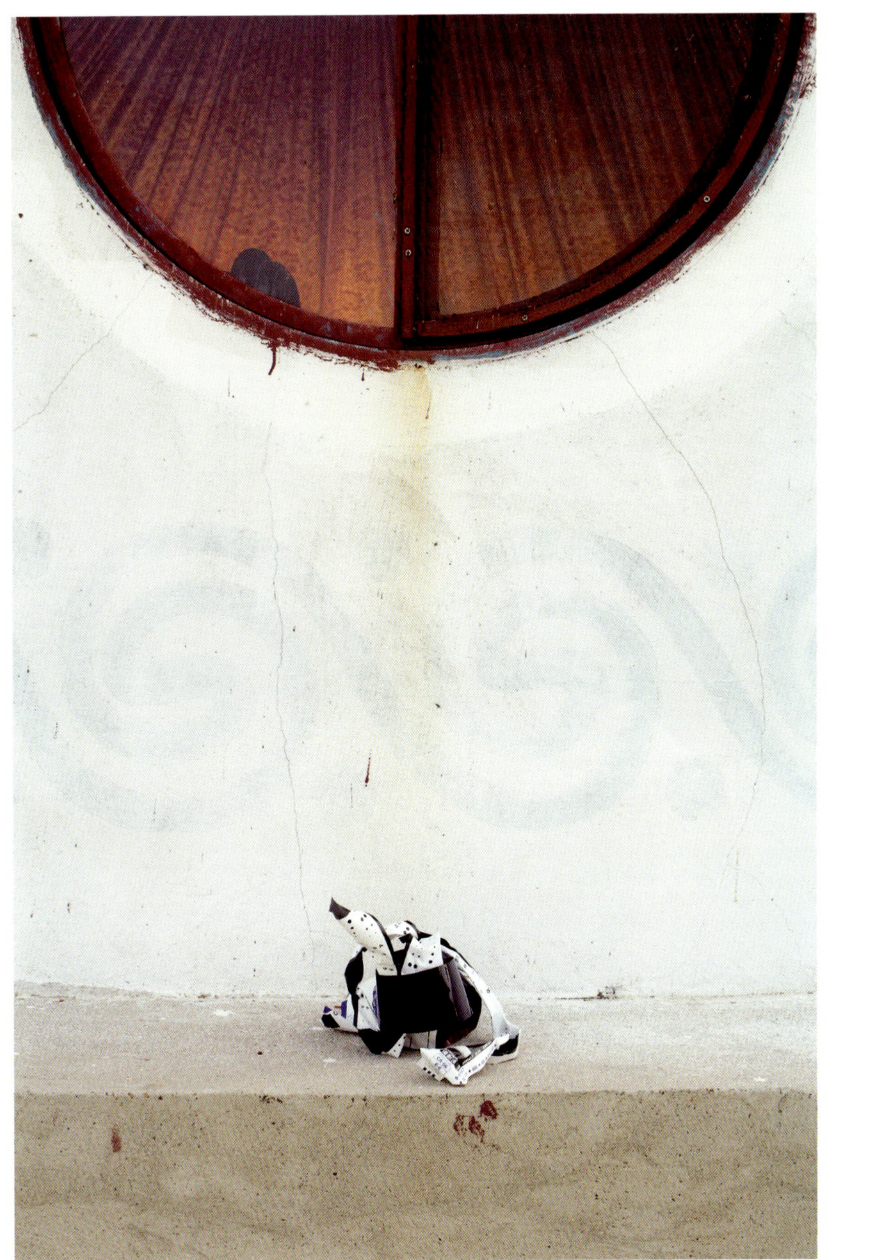

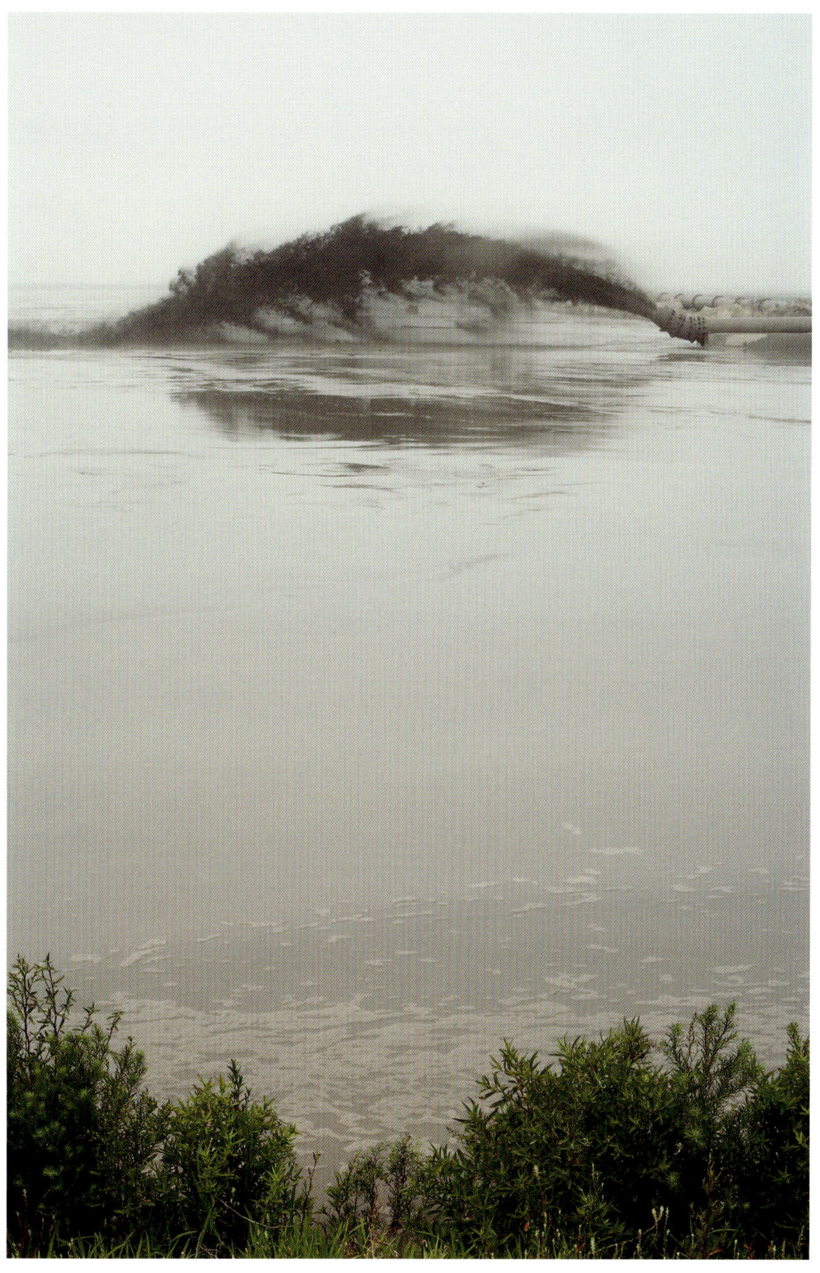

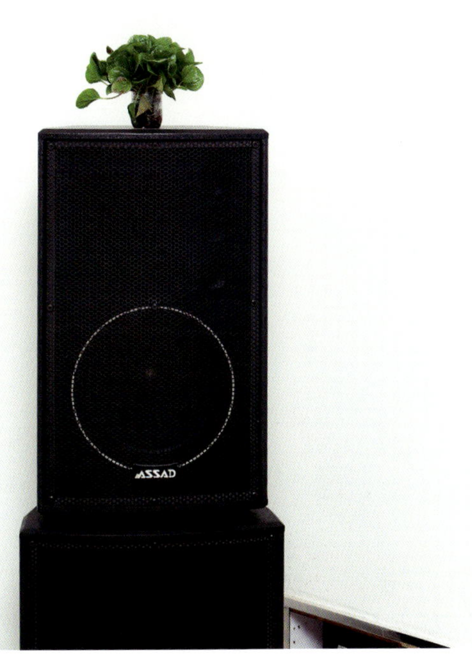

ASSAD

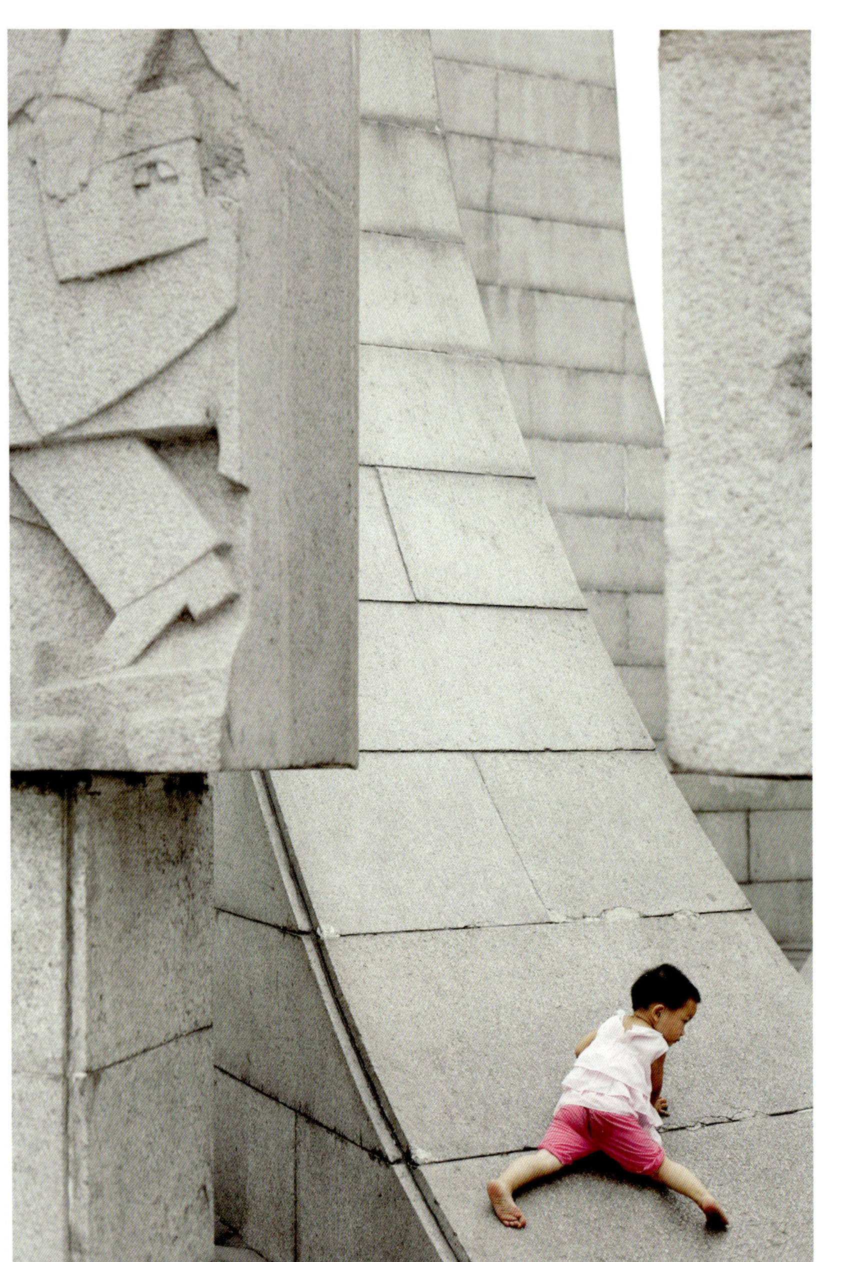

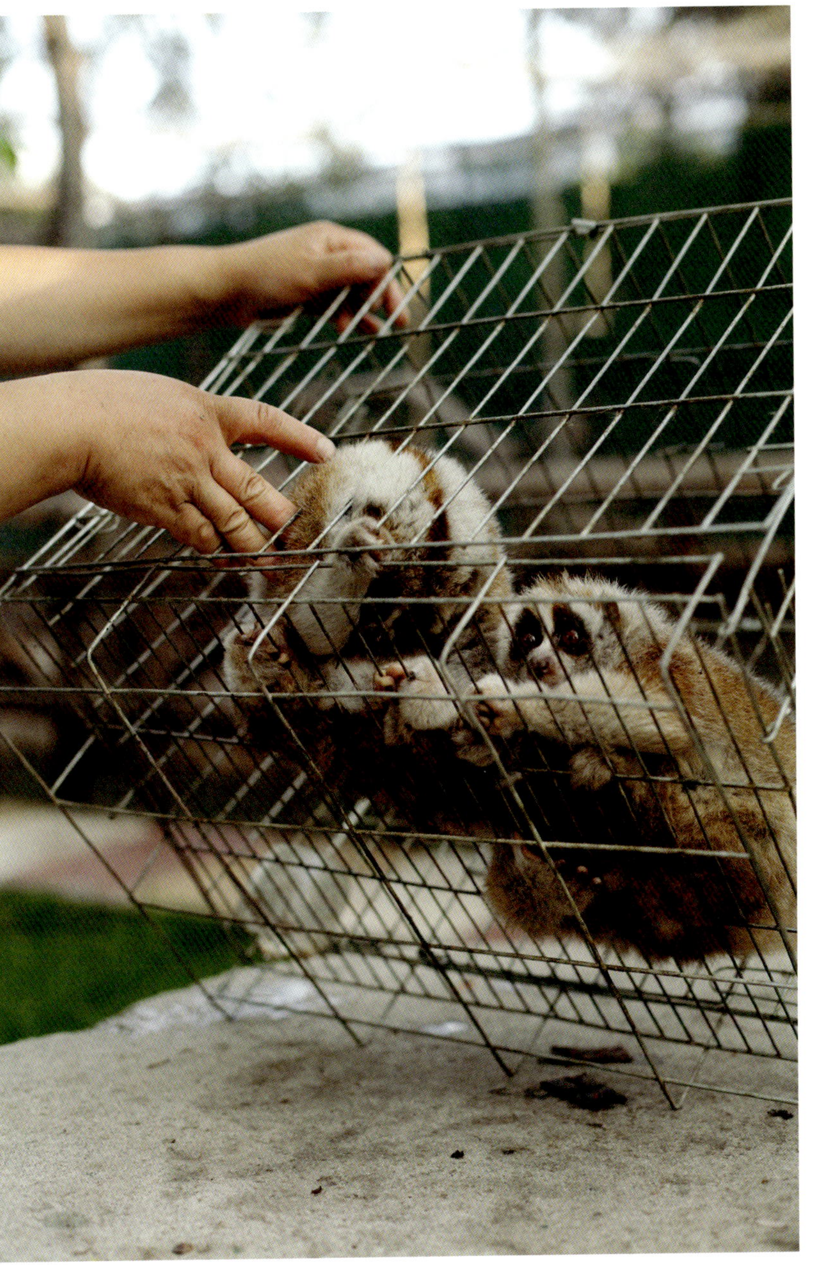

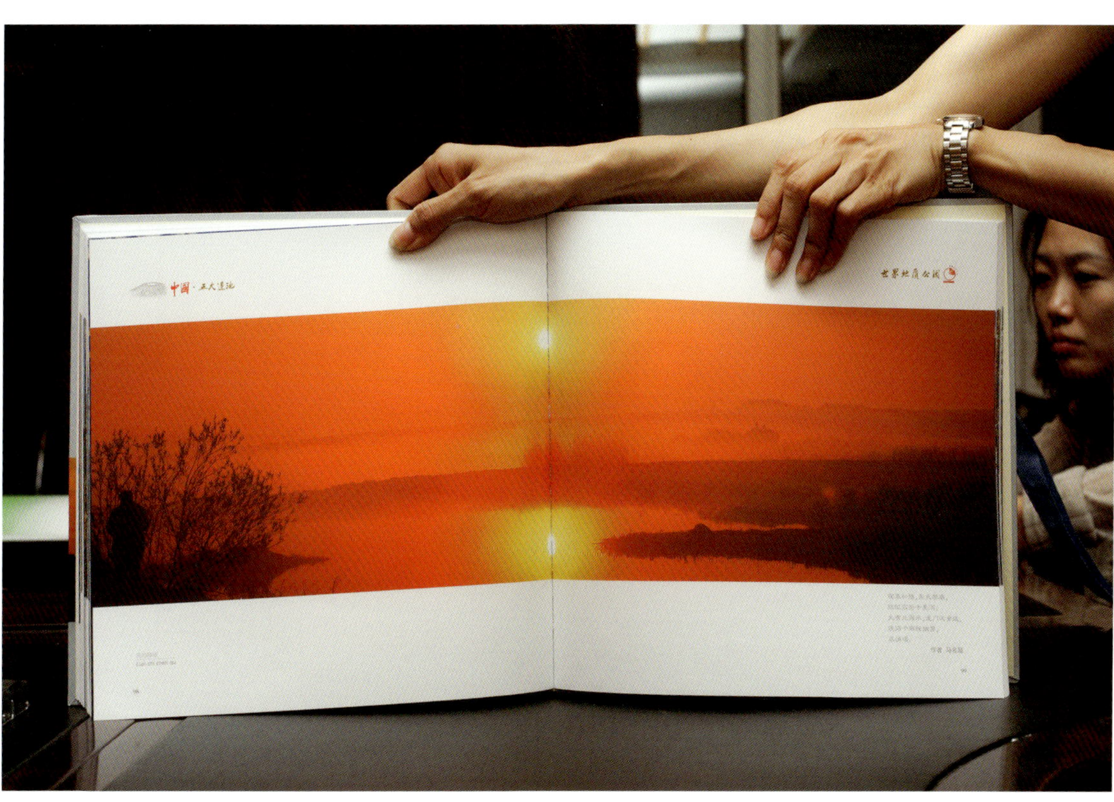

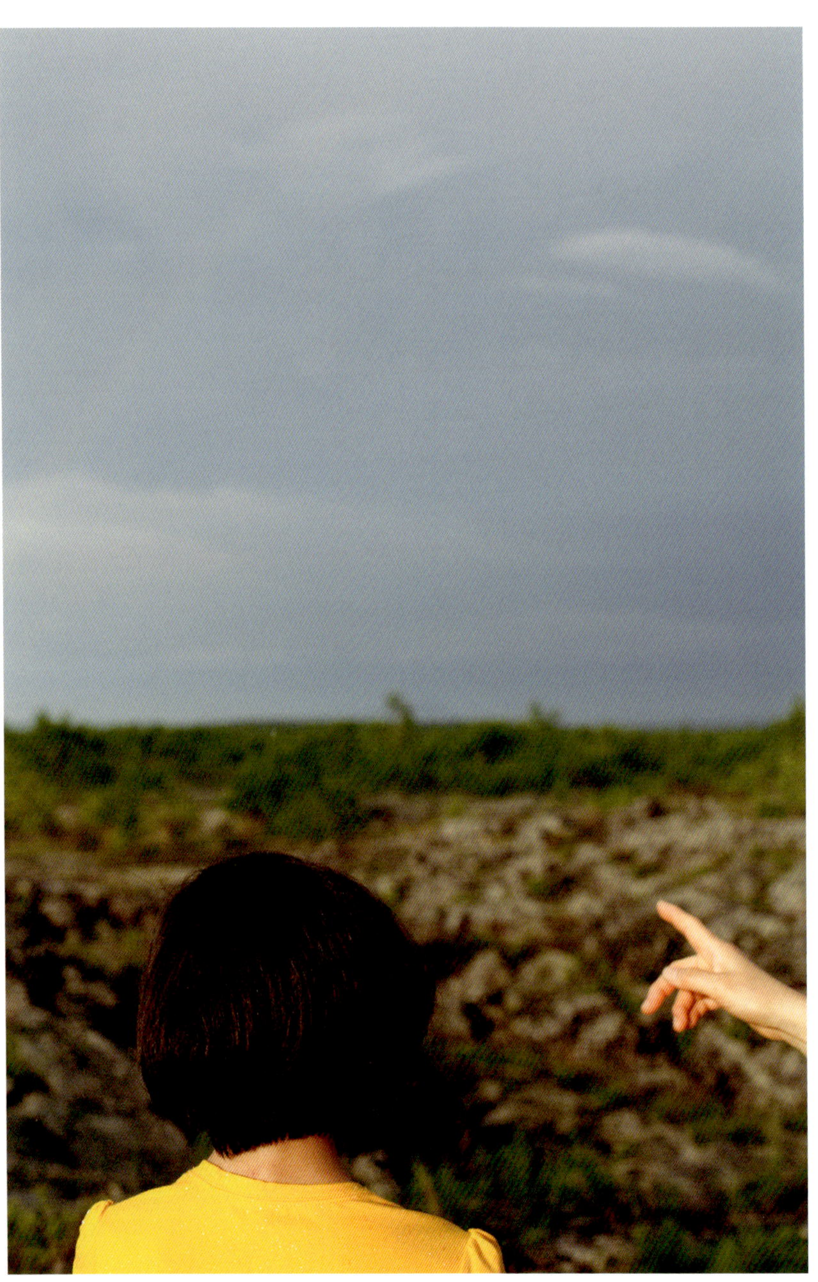

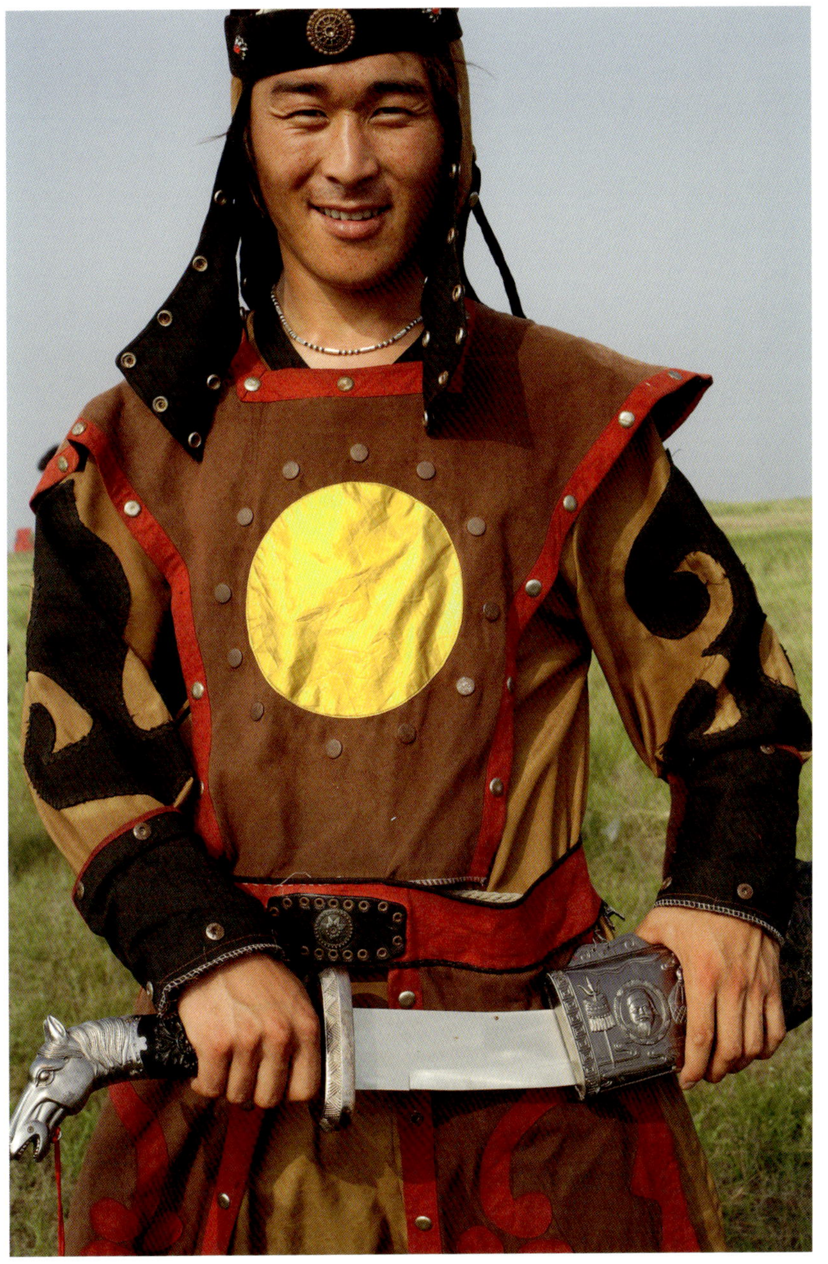

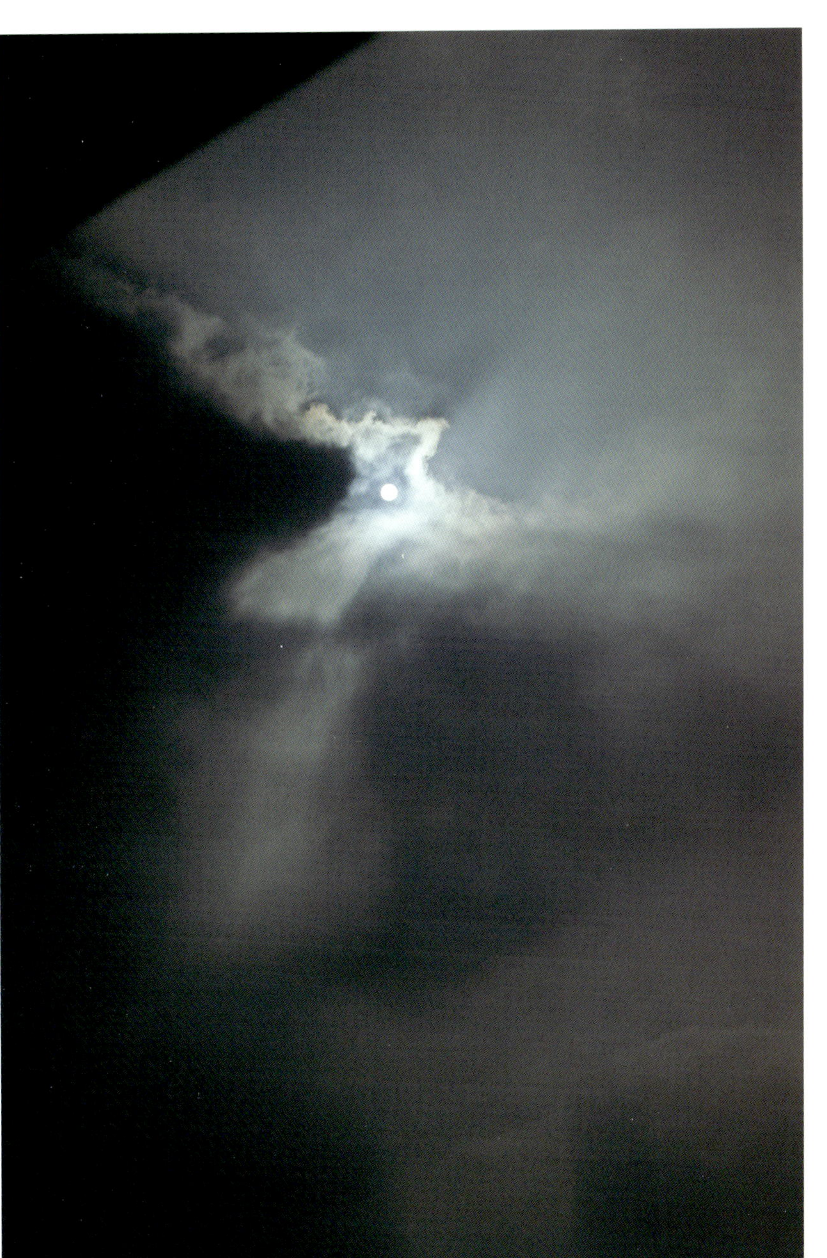

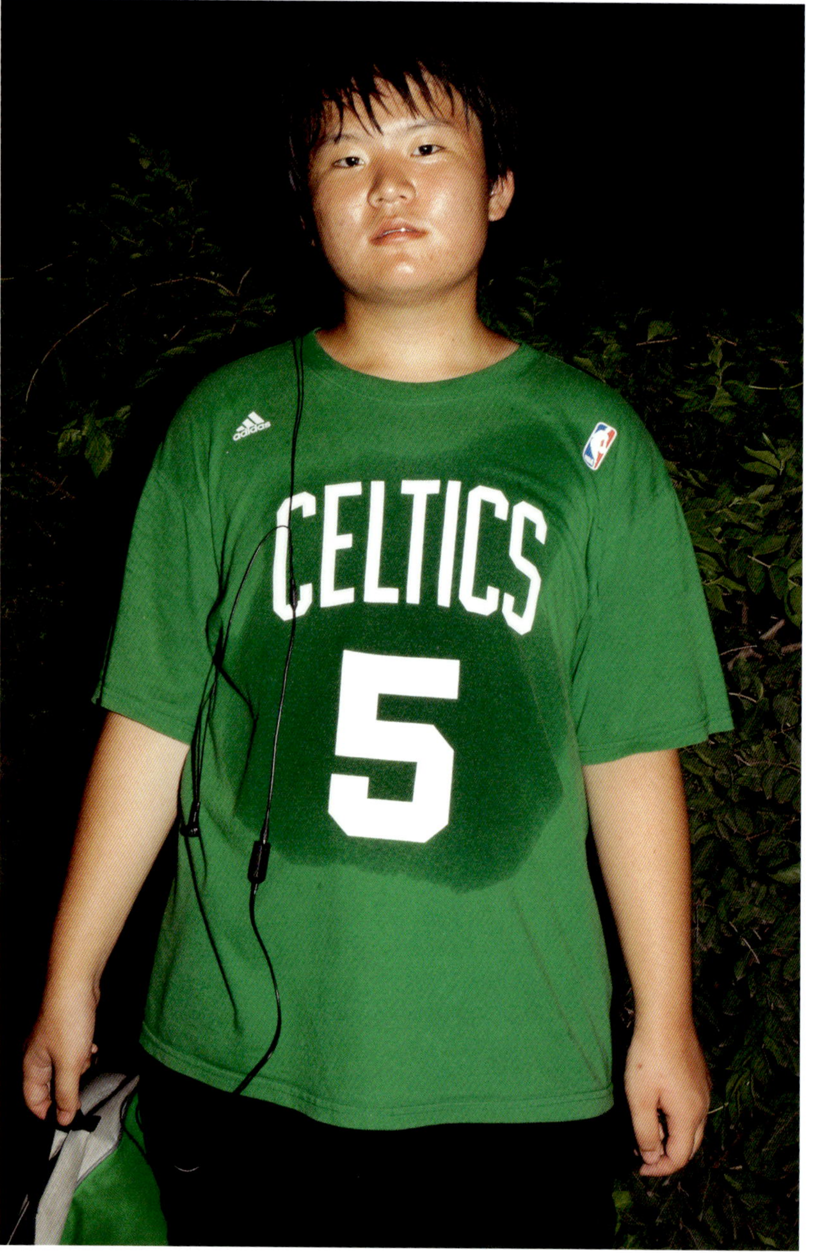

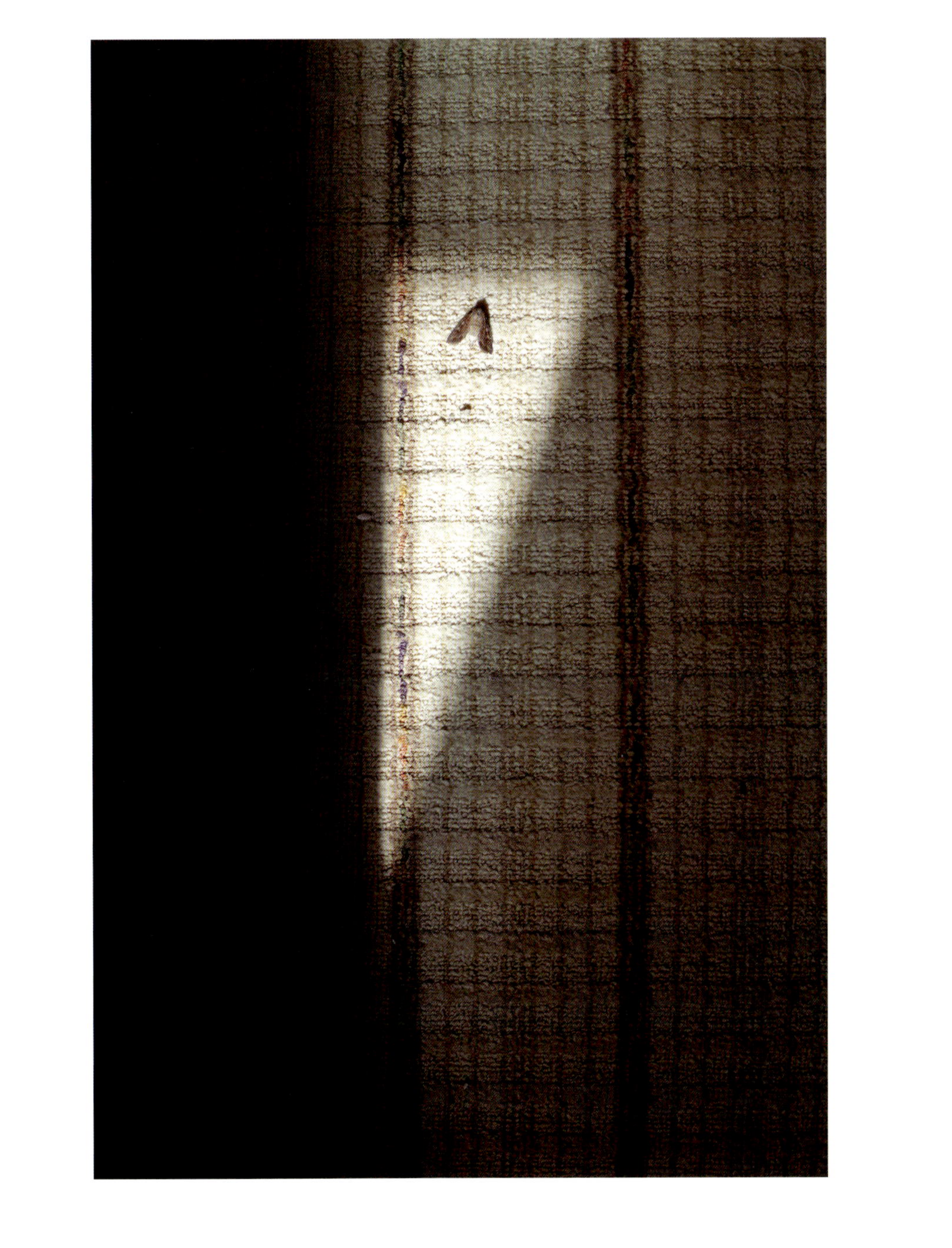

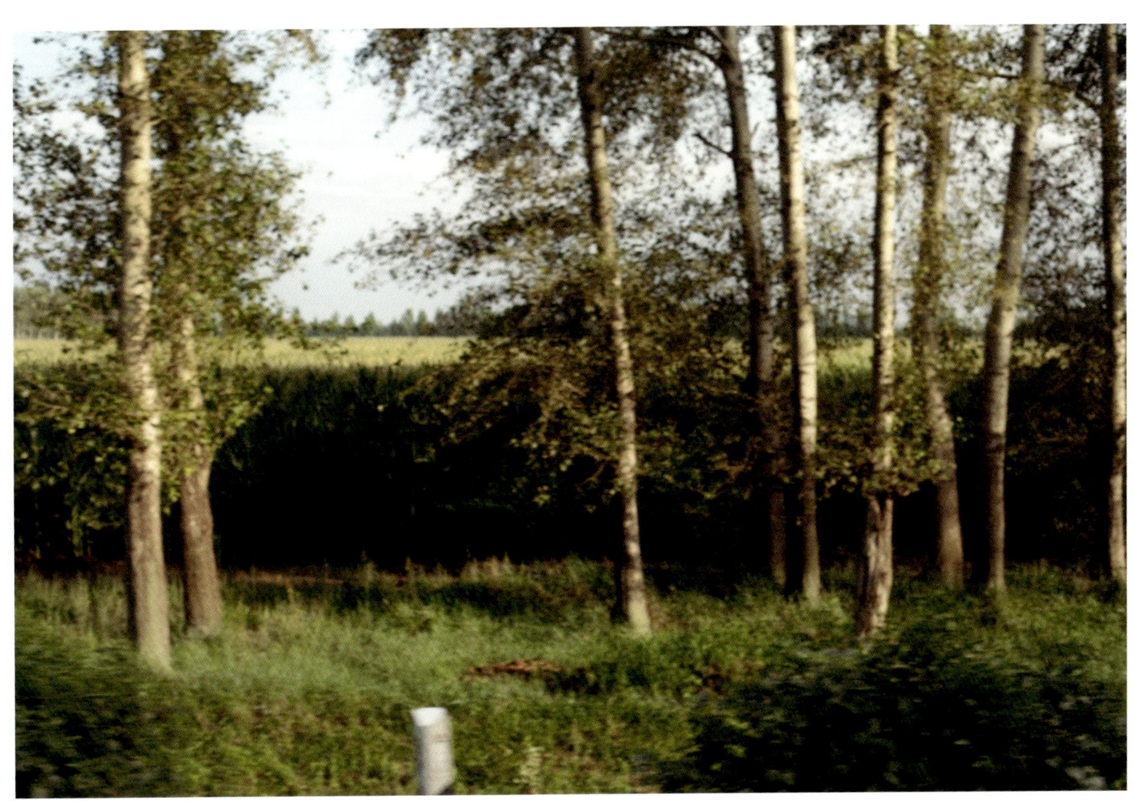

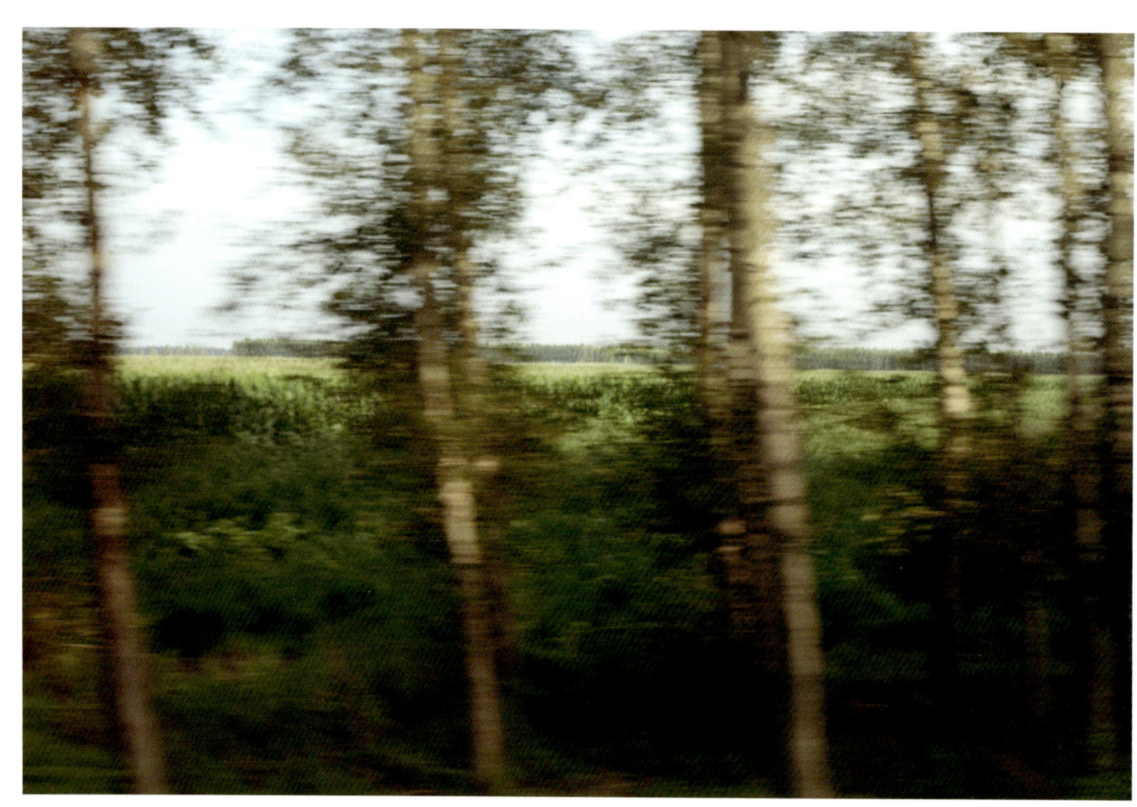

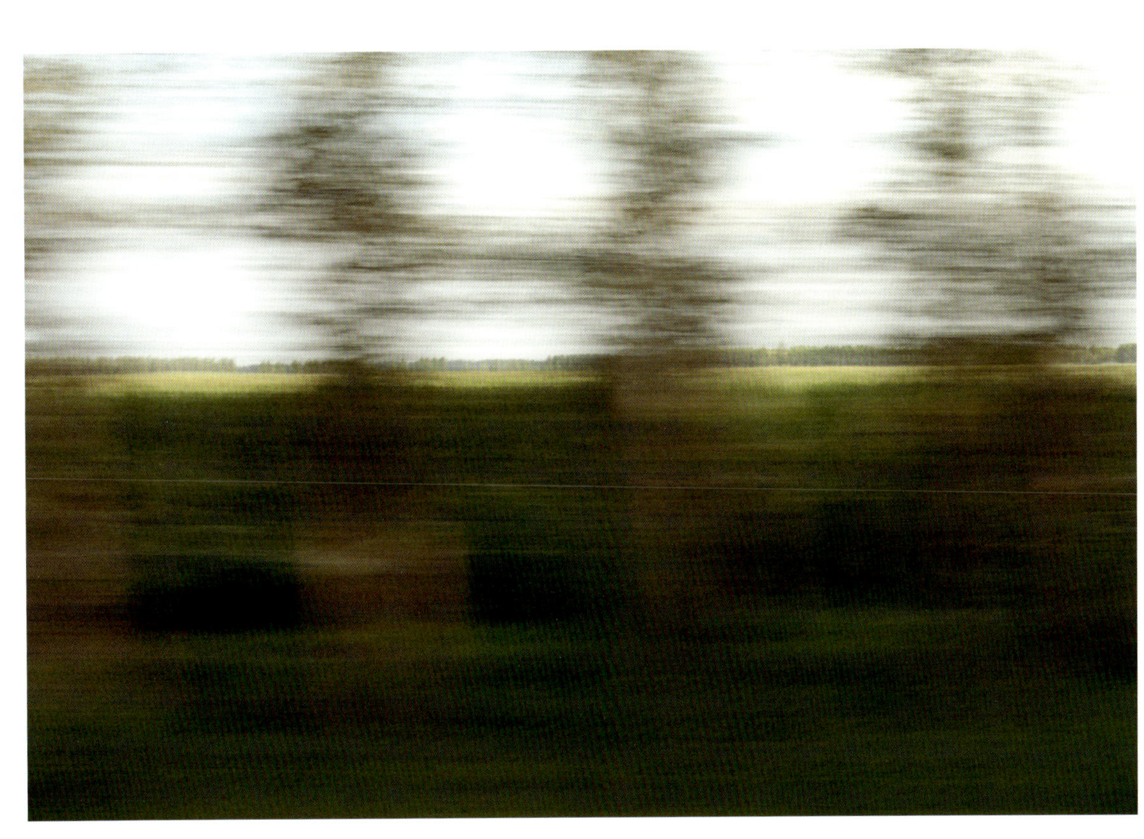

zuijing guantian: "like looking at the sky from the bottom of a well."

FROM THE BOTTOM OF A WELL
Publication © 2011 Shawn Records and A-Jump Books
Photographs © 2011 Shawn Records (2010)

Published by A-Jump Books, Ithaca, NY
Printed by Oddi Printing, Reykjavik, Iceland
Edition of 500
First Printing

Thanks:
Ron Jude, Danielle Mericle, Alexis Pike, Doug Dubois, Yan Li, High Noon
Culture, Laura Moya & Photolucida past and present, Matthew Stadler,
Rachel Shapiro, Leah Jacobson, Grant Olsen, Ralf Youtz, Light Work,
and of course Sam, Max, Jenny and the rest of the family.

ISBN 978-0-9777655-7-7

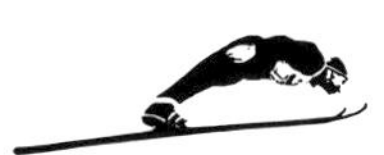

A-JUMP BOOKS
www.a-jumpbooks.com
info@a-jumpbooks.com

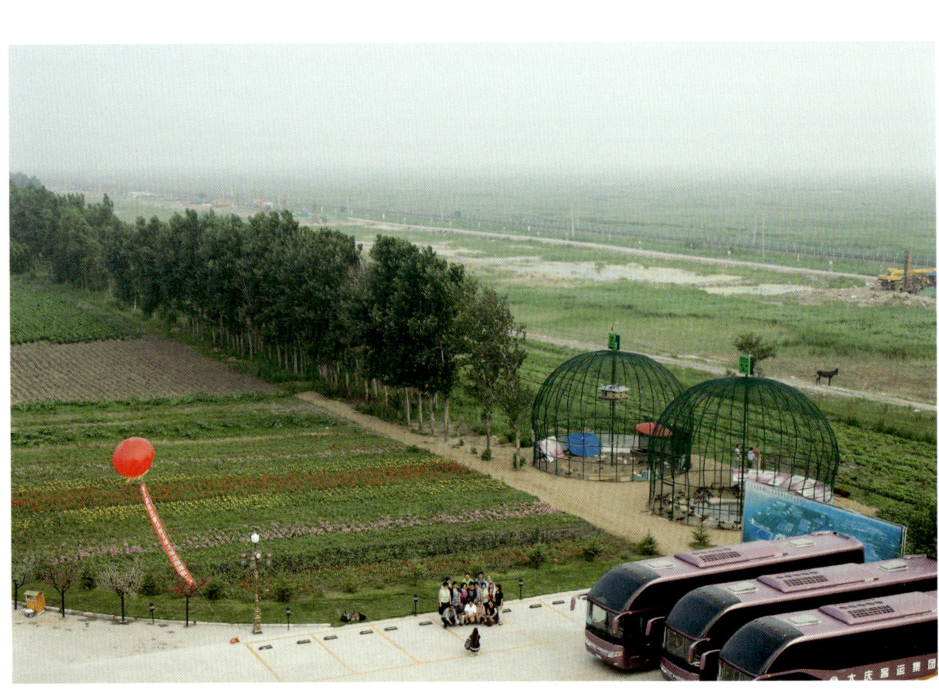